Tendons & Tendrils

David Blunk, II

BookLeaf
Publishing

India | USA | UK

Presentation by *BookLeaf Publishing*

Web: www.bookleafpub.com

E-mail: info@bookleafpub.com

ISBN: 9789363300767

First edition 2024

ACKNOWLEDGEMENT

My mother told me to pick the very best one, and you are not it.

Also:
--Cedric Tai, for your collaboration on LEAVING LOVE.
--William Munn & Rebecca Scheer, educators who have left an impression since high school.
--Joseph Combs, for helping me through the transition to hometown life.

PREFACE

Though it is hard to be a king, it is harder yet to become one. This is especially true if among those who are to be your subjects and in international opinion it is generally accepted that you are not quite in your right mind, and are some sort of bloody idiot who repeatedly does stunning, inexplicable things that embarrass your wife, your family, and the nation--but not you, because you believe, and state, that you are impeccably sane, and you cannot understand what all the fuss is about.

You refuse embarrassment because you hold that kings and those who would be kings must struggle to find and define their duty and their special place in the world, and are meant to live on the edge. Why do people expect kings to be unlike anyone else, and then punish them for it? Why is a king, who by accident of birth must submit to the will and expectation of scores of millions, or even (as is the case of the British, world-apparent monarchy) thousands of millions, savagely held to account as he forges a tormented youth into what must appear on

Coronation Day to be a royal being of evident perfection?

Like a Roman gladiator alternately reviled by or beloved of the crowd, prior to his ascension to the throne the future king lives a life of overwrought luxury, dreadful isolation, and constant challenge. He desires above all to be an ordinary man, if only because a king is kept from the world as ordinary men are not, and the world is an inestimably better and richer prize than any throne. And yet he will fight savagely to achieve his destiny, not because it is attractive to him but because his sense of honour will not let him desert the field. How strange.

But that is theory, and this is the story not only of the royal state but of two people, Freddy and Fredericka, who had to come to terms both with it and with each other. After so many articles in the press and years of frothy gossip, you may think you know them, but you don't.

My account of what befell them is as unvarnished and pure as a tree on an ocean promontory that has been stripped of its leaves in storm, or a sheep that has been shorn to the pink. It is brutally, literally, and mortifyingly true. This is not because iI hold no brief for those two dear friends but because I was asked--commanded--to present their story without argument, polemic, defence, or excuse. For the most part it is a story that I know only as it was told to me. how do I know then, and how can I assure others, that it is accurate?

I know because I was present at the many hypnosis sessions at Sandringham, during which I was absolutely sure that the king was not pretending, for as brilliant and versatile as he may be, he does not have other than in the hypnotic state the ability to read, memorise, and recite backward the Karachi Yellow Pages at high speed, all the while simulating with intense bodily jerkings the paroxysmal dath struggle of a salt-water game fish. I know because I used every means to verify all that was related to me, and I know because I have it on the word of someone who has suffered mightily for the sake of such things as keeping his word. But I know most of all because it was told to me, bereft of embellishment, as a duty of the heart and in memory of one who is gone.

I do admit to having taken some liberties of narration. How else could I convey the scope both of their adventures and their transformation? But you cannot trust me, you must trust only the story. I myself am but a cipher to their great account, and what follows is not mine but theirs. And, when you enter, you will be not with me, but with them most certainly. Imagine, therefore, that within these paper portals is an ancient monarchy brought to a parlous state, and a warlike and restless prince lost in a time that for its lack of passion, modesty, and truth was inappropriate to him and broke his heart again and again, but could never break it all the way.

GEOFFREY, LORD PIGGLESWADE
Gower Lodge, Mortlake

Freddy and Fredericka, Mark Helprin, 2005

TWINE MEDITATION

This morning, a piece of twine presented itself to
me.

Sinuous, ascetic in its visual elegance, it flew
past my face, and floated in the wind as I sipped
my strong coffee on my fire escape.

I contemplated keeping my distance, keeping it
as a memory, but I reached out and grasped it.

It wound 400 times around my four fingers,
before finally becoming taught.

I never found out what it was attached to, but I
still do wonder.
As I unwound the string, I said aloud the names
of those I've lost.

It started to rain--just a light sprinkle, a dusting,
a joke, really.

I buried the ball of twine, still connected to its
mysterious source, into the soil of this
houseplant I've been working on; I killed one,
then planted some seeds as a hope for continuity.
They've since sprouted.

When I came home, after running some
Saturday errands around an empty yet antsy city,
I checked on my new friend.

There was a small divot in the soil.
New sprouts.
The ball of twine is gone.

--Drafted during the COVID-19 pandemic,
August 29, 2020.

FORGIVENESS

It's for myself
It's elusive
It's multifactor
It's hard
It's a hotbutton topic

It's in-process
It's farsighted

Forgiveness
It's gotten easier with age
It's helped me to grow
Forgiveness
Something happened
I knew it, my parents knew it, my grandparents
knew it
Nobody did anything.
Nobody had repercussions
Cycles were not stopped
My growth almost was
She was a child, herself
From a broken home
A product of abuse
Not her fault
Not mine

Forgiveness

TENDONS

5

They don't break,

They snap.
Back into shape.

CICADAS & SUNSETS

She told me:

Go out
Put your feet on the earth
Get into nature.

Get grounded.

Living in the present moment
Has taught me to appreciate the chaos as well as
the serenity.
Cicadas and sunsets no longer make me run.

I tell you:

Go out.

Outside of yourself
Outside of your comfort
Outside of your history

Give thanks to Nature. Express your gratitude at
the end of every day.

CHAOS MEDITATION

Chaos & Calm
So close together, yet at times polar opposites.

When you've spent your life
Making lists
Keeping track
Keeping score,

A change of plans or unpredictable comment can
cut deeply enough to
Flay,
to fray.

BELOVED, remember:
That initial chaotic frazzle is
TEMPORARY.

YOU are on the other side of that wall.

Now climb it.

TENDRILS

Reaching out
Grasping for a support system

I found my roots once again,
In the familiar streets, faces of my hometown.

Moving home, I've begun to
Flourish

With another day's sun, I'm able to unfurl my
leaves, stretch my vines
Seeking light, and nourishment

While I'm still lonely
While I'm still recovering
While I'm still in treatment

I am grateful

For this opportunity

To grow.

SYMPATHY & EMPATHY

Radical generosity
Inspires gratitude.

In order to grow both, understand:
You can have either, or.
But cultivating them
Takes time.

Sympathy: NOUN;
1: feelings of pity and sorrow for someone else's
misfortune.
2: understanding between people; common
feeling.

Empathy: NOUN;
1: the ability to understand and share the
feelings of another.

CREATIVITY MEDITATION

Thank you,
Higher Power.

That's the name I'll use.
Thank you, for allowing me to be grateful for
today.

A day where I woke up slowly, and with
intention, listing my gratitudes in my head,
while listening to the birds and feeling the
breeze from outside my Bedroom window,
Watching the sunlight filter, scatter, and shower
rainbows and bright light all Around me.

I am so safe, these days. Protected by my
family's love, my love for myself, and my desire
for a great and happy future.

I have a beautiful, safe place to rest my head. I
have nourishment. I have time--Time to learn,
time to grow, and time to do the things for
myself that allow me to Operate at my best.

Time to get up, stretch the body, take the medication which helps my brain to work normally, consult today's schedule, and insert some creativity.

TENDONS II

Sarah had always been a resilient and strong-willed woman. Growing up in a low-income household in the bustling city of New York, she had learned from a young age to fend for herself and never give up, no matter how tough life got. However, the events of 2023 would test her strength in ways she never thought possible.

It all started when Sarah received an eviction notice from her landlord. Due to unforeseen circumstances, she had fallen behind on her rent payments and was unable to come up with the money in time. Devastated and feeling defeated, she packed up her few belongings and found herself homeless on the unforgiving streets of New York.

As if things couldn't get any worse, Sarah received news that her closest friend had passed away suddenly. The loss hit her hard, and she found herself spiraling into a deep pit of despair and hopelessness. In her grief, she turned to substance use as a way to numb the pain and escape reality.

One night, after a particularly heavy drinking session, Sarah found herself in the emergency room, having overdosed on alcohol. It was a wake-up call for her, a harsh reminder of how out of control her life had become. It was in that hospital bed that Sarah made a vow to herself – to turn her life around and find a way out of the darkness.

Over the next few months, Sarah went through a grueling journey of self-discovery and healing. She attended therapy sessions, joined support groups, and sought out resources for homeless individuals in the city. It was a long and arduous process, but Sarah was determined to reclaim her life and rebuild herself from the ground up.

As she began to heal emotionally and mentally, Sarah also started to pay more attention to her physical health. She started working out at a local gym, pushing her body to its limits and feeling the rush of endorphins that came with each workout. It was during one of these sessions that she thought about the strength of tendons in the body – how they connect muscle to bone and provide support and stability.

Sarah saw a parallel between the tendons in her body and her own strength and resilience. Just like the tendons, she had been tested and stretched to her limits, but she had never broken. Instead, she had grown stronger and more resilient, just like those ligaments connecting her muscles.

Through the process of rebuilding her life, Sarah learned the importance of self-love, self-acceptance, and setting boundaries. She realized that she was worthy of love and respect, and that she didn't have to rely on substances to cope with her pain. She also learned how to set boundaries with others, to protect her own well-being and prioritize her mental and emotional health.

As the months went by, Sarah began to see a transformation in herself. No longer the broken and lost woman she once was, she stood tall and proud, a beacon of strength and resilience. She had overcome the eviction, the loss of her friend, homelessness, substance use, and hospitalization, and had emerged on the other side stronger and more determined than ever.

Today, Sarah continues to thrive in the city that once brought her so much pain. She has found a stable job, a safe place to live, and a supportive community that she can rely on. She knows that life will always have its ups and downs, but she also knows that she has the strength and resilience to face whatever comes her way.

As Sarah looks back on her journey, she is reminded of the tendons in her body – the strong and resilient connections that have supported her through her darkest days. Just like those ligaments, she has grown and stretched, but she has never broken. And she knows that as long as she continues to nurture and care for herself, she will continue to grow stronger.

Just like those ligaments connecting her muscles.

Written with AI, August 2024.

DOGS & BABIES

When I look at a dog's eyes, I see a world of
innocence and unconditional love.
Pure and genuine.

Babies, on the other hand, are like little bundles
of joy and wonder.

Their heightened senses and displays of
affection mesmerize us.

Truly a gift, dogs & babies make me grateful for
every day of joy and inspiration they bring to
life.

SATURDAY MEDITATION

The strong breeze
The dappled bedroom light
Noticing new backyard garden growth

The simplest gesture
Sharing a meal, cooked with love
Whether dining together or on my own

I will treasure these moments

These are why I moved home.

NOW IS YOUR TIME

A simple post-it note
On the wall of an office
Changed my day.

"Now is your time,"
it reads. Day-glo orange.

It stopped me in my tracks.
In a lot of ways, I am simply unable to discern
the sentiment.

I am temporarily disabled.
Recovering from 2023.
Funny to think of how much has changed, in
almost a year;

I know I can have a meal when hungry.
My bills paid, my hierarchy of needs mostly
met.

PERHAPS, NOW IS YOUR TIME.

THIRTEEN

13 chances to change my mind.

12 days into my first hospitalization, last year,
was when I decided to move home.

11 is another number that I see, constantly. I
notice the time, when it passes 11:11AM and
11:11PM.

10 minutes to meditate lowers blood pressure
and eases headaches, cortisol levels, and stress.

9 PM is wind-down time. Every night.

8 minutes, to walk down to the pond.
Remember that.

7 another number I see often.

6 is an angelic number, number of Raguel, an
Arcangel.

5 senses to ground me. What do you smell?
What do you see? What do you hear? What do
you physically feel? What do you taste?

4 souls, under one roof: myself, my mother, and
our two familiar dogs: Zander and Porkchop.

3 another number I see often, indicative of the
Christian holy trinity.

2 mental health hospitalizations in one year was
quite enough.

1 me. One life. Time to shine.

UNTITLED

22

That sanguine, robust red.
The most valiant of purples.
The most unsettling shade of chartreuse.

I saw these colors, before last night's sleep.
I see them once more, as 1968 flashes before my
eyes with abandon.

That sanguine, robust red.
The most valiant of purples.
The most unsettling shade of chartreuse.

LEAVING LOVE

Originally published in a small press literary
journal, REFLECTIONS, by Project UP,
Marion, Indiana, 2002.

Where do we go from here,
Now that love has left us fractured?
Do we sit and mumble like grumpy old men?
Sit and wine like children?
Stand up like heroes?
Or, do we let time pass by like Old Man River?

Where do we go from here, now that love has
left us torn,
Divided like countries with fire and brimstone
boundaries?
Why men rarely cry...
Was it better to have loved and lost than never
loved at all?
Or, is it better being the Jolly Blind Monk?

Fear, predetermination,
An expectation.
Proposed mental and physical strength.

Bunk.

Men cry. Women cry.
Everything has a time of sadness.

A river.

The metaphor of the situation.
You on one bank, I the other.

A space, ever changing, inbetween.
Do I jump in,
Rekindle?
Or watch it sweep away emotion?

Either way, it comes, it goes, it flows... Will I
find another?
Was there another?
Would you have told me?
Do I still love you? What went wrong?

That which went wrong is our perception of our
love, a
Feeling of necessity of change.

So where do we go from here, now that love has
left us

Fractured, torn, bruised, numb, sensitive,
delirious, doubtful,
Hopeless, and weak?
Where, exactly?

Maybe fate came too soon. Maybe fate has
already happened.

In the end I'm standing here waiting for you.
Sometimes I'm
Sitting with my hand on my cheek, going to the
same places we
Used to go, and all I remember is you.
Because there's no place like...YOU.

But do you try? Do you try at all?
It's time to try something.
There's no place like you, but is that a place I
need to be right
Now?

So here goes, I'm moving on.

I packed the moving van with my heart, my
mind is at the
Steering wheel. I can't tell if you're waving
goodbye or
Flipping me off, it will all be a blur...

Here goes. Hello world, I live. I guess there is
life after love,
But the price is... Priceless.

I move on.

Without you.

But then, you come back...

Ah, bliss! Dual epiphanies!

Um, thanks...

I forgot my hat.

--David S. Blunk, II & Cedric Tai

UNTITLED II

I'd bottle today's feeling, if I could. To still
have a supply,
on my not-so-good days.

First, let's recap last night: my porkchops, au
gratin potatoes, and stuffing were a hit; made me
want to offer to handle dinner today, too.
Alli's visit with Jasper – 3rd in a row—went,
"Amazing," in her words. Fine by us, too! I had
an excellent night, last night, ending with texting
with Kaicy more, and making plans for Tuesday.
Today was my second day, waking up at a more
reasonable time. I enjoyed it!
I also did yoga—great little streak developing!

I also made progress on my unclaimed funds, as
well as on the Hartford. Shelby came by to talk
with Mom about her injured cat. Got him to the
vet.

I prioritized doing my reading this morning;
along with some paperwork. Then I vacuumed
the whole house. Had a little bit of a manic
cleaning attack, as I do. Made meatloaf

(bomb!), mashed potatoes (Dad made), and carrots for dinner. AMAZING.

Enjoyed spending wind-down Jasper time, with the family. Got to kiss him goodnight.

Now it's time to bubble-bathe and read, as I do, and get some early good rest, for tomorrow's sake. Thanks be to HIGHER POWER for a great, normal-feeling, to me, day.

--Journal entry, 19 May 2024.

HOMELANDER

This book is a tool.

It's the first I've published since high school. A long time coming!

Please remember to keep it handy, and to thumb through it, occasionally. Not only will it remind you of the positivity of 2024, Dear, but it will also help you to ground yourself, to stay mindful and in the present moment. What a gift!

You've given this gift to yourself. Never forget that.

LONELINESS
MEDITATION

This book is a tool.

It's the first I've published since high school. A long time coming!

Please remember to keep it handy, and to thumb through it, occasionally. Not only will it remind you of the positivity of 2024, Dear, but it will also help you to ground yourself, to stay mindful and in the present moment. What a gift!

You've given this gift to yourself. Never forget that.

Noticing the end of an era
Looking forward to things changing.
Anticipating
Anticipation.

ALMOST A YEAR

For almost a year, I've been sitting here
Re-learning how to live.
For almost a year, I've had some real fear

Of connection, self-sabotage, that I haven't
enough to give.

For almost a year, I've been sitting here
Adjusting to this return
While it's taken some time, I've crafted a rhyme

And my wounds and scars no longer burn.

For almost a year, I've been sitting here
Filled with utter joy
The kind you only dream about, when you're a
little boy.

For almost a year, I've made it clear,

That my time's not a thing to waste; With a
meaningful stare,

Or the flick of a thumb, I'll put you in your
place.

For almost a year, I've felt, right here,

In the upper left part of my chest,

A pumping, a beating, a begging, a pleading

"SEE? YOU'RE AT PEACE."

PORKCHOP

For over a decade
We've shared lives
We've shared beds

You're my silent steed
My anxiety-pressure-valve
My soothsayer and stress reliever

I am SO HAPPY to see your health improving,
maintaining. My awkward dog.

You did the hard work of protecting me, keeping
me safe, homeless on the streets of New York.

Now, let me remember, every day, that you've
earned your "retirement."

I'll try to give you the best of the best.

THANK YOU.

Poem 21

Twenty one, and now we're done.

Thanks are due to BOOKLEAF PUBLISHING, for participating in this challenge. I'm so happy to have the opportunity to memorialize a particularly trying time, in my life. Onward and upward, from here!

#thewriteangle
#thewriteangle2024

9 789363 300767